Find the Mistakes
Science Adventures

Wonders of the Wild

Written by Q.L. Pearce
Illustrated by Greg Battes

Reviewed and endorsed by:
Theresa Prator
Curatorial Assistant
Los Angeles Zoo

With special thanks to:
Tony Valenzuela
Curator of Mammals
Los Angeles Zoo

Copyright ©1990 by RGA Publishing Group, Inc.
Published by Price Stern Sloan, Inc.
360 North La Cienega Blvd., Los Angeles, CA 90048

ISBN: 0-8431-2815-1

10 9 8 7 6 5 4 3 2 1

PRICE STERN SLOAN, INC.
Los Angeles

Giraffe

Strange as it may seem, a giraffe has the same number of bones in its remarkably long neck as you do! Humans and giraffes, just like most mammals, have seven neck bones, or vertebrae (VER-tuh-bray), but each of the giraffe's neck bones is very long. At least nine different kinds of giraffes live in Africa. Each type has a different number of short, fur-covered horns—from two to five—and a unique pattern of spots.

The world's tallest animal, the giraffe may reach a height of 18 feet or more from the ground to the tip of its horns. Long, slender legs add to the giraffe's stature. Its belly may be as much as six feet off the ground. That's tall enough for most humans to walk under without stooping!

The giraffe uses its 18-inch-long tongue to grasp twigs and pull tasty leaves from the branches of acacia (uh-KAY-shuh) and wild apricot trees. Because of its height, this graceful animal can reach leaves that other browsers cannot. But being tall isn't always a plus for the giraffe, especially when it's thirsty. Surprisingly, the animal's neck is not long enough to reach down to a water hole. To get a drink of water, the giraffe must first spread its front legs wide. This way, it can stoop its shoulders and head low enough to get a drink.

Can you find and color 16 mistakes?

Okapi

Have you ever tried to touch the tip of your nose with your tongue? The okapi's tongue is so long that it can lick its own ears! The okapi is a shy relative of the giraffe, but it lives in the African jungle instead of on the grasslands. Like its grassland cousin, the okapi has front legs that are much longer than its hind legs. At the shoulder, the okapi is as tall as a human. This height allows the okapi to browse easily on the leaves and twigs of trees. It can weigh up to 500 pounds, or nearly three times the weight of an average man. Its short, sleek coat is deep purple-brown, and light and dark stripes ring its legs. Males have a pair of tiny, fur-covered horns.

Scientists find studying the okapi a challenge. Usually alone, the okapi lives hidden in the shadows of a small area of African forest that is difficult to reach. Still, we do know a little about its behavior. Although timid around humans, okapis can be pushy with each other. Males fight for mates by pushing and shoving. Rivals approach each other with heads lowered. Each tries to maneuver its head under the other animal's neck, and the successful animal shoves its opponent's head violently upward.

Can you find and color 16 mistakes?

Cheetah

The fastest living land mammal, the amazing cheetah can rocket to speeds of over 60 miles per hour in just a few seconds. On the attack, this member of the cat family is an astonishing sight. First, the cheetah slowly edges near a victim, perhaps a young antelope. Then, suddenly, it springs forward. Using its long, slender tail as a counterbalance, the cheetah twists and turns. Racing after its fleeing prey, it closes the gap between them, covering up to 23 feet in a single stride. But the cheetah can't keep up this grueling speed. If the antelope can stay ahead in the race for 400 hundred yards or so, it survives. In that distance, the cheetah tires and gives up. Although an excellent hunter, the cheetah must often try several times before it finally captures a meal.

With its straw-colored, black-spotted coat, the seven-foot-long cheetah looks a little like a slim leopard. But it differs from the leopard and other great cats. While the leopard and tiger hunt at night, the cheetah is most active during the day. There are other differences, too. The cheetah's claws do not retract completely, as do the claws of all the other great cats, and the pupils of its eyes are round instead of narrow.

Can you find and color 12 mistakes?

Black Rhinoceros

The black rhinoceros is the trailblazer of the African bush country. Dense, thorny brush isn't a barrier to a rhinoceros if there's water on the other side. The thorns are no match for the black rhino's tough hide, and the huge beast simply crashes straight through. Before long, other animals begin to use the convenient trail the rhino has made.

The rhinoceros never roams far from a source of water, for it drinks at least once a day. In the dry season, it may dig for water with its front feet. But it's not just looking for water—it also needs mud! Wallowing in thick mud helps the black rhino to stay cool and to rid itself of ticks and flies. It also gets rid of ticks and flies with the help of a small bird called an oxpecker. This bird rides on the rhino's back, dining on the parasites as it goes.

At 12 feet long and one and a half tons, the black rhinoceros looks a little like a battle tank with a slim tail. A fringe of coarse hair trims its small ears, and its pointed, flexible upper lip is perfect for tugging the leaves it eats from thorny bushes. But its most remarkable feature is its two heavy horns. The rear horn is short and stout, while the curved front horn may be up to four feet long.

Can you find and color 13 mistakes?

Spotted Hyena

Of all the sounds that fill the African night, the eerie call of the spotted hyena may be the most chilling. Sounding almost like crazed laughter, this call means that a kill has been made. It is an invitation for other hyenas to join in the feast. This strange call gave the animal its nickname: the "laughing" hyena.

The powerful, five-foot-long spotted hyena, largest of the hyena family, resembles a dog, but it is more closely related to the mongoose or civet. It has a strongly sloping back, rounded ears, pale, coarse fur flecked with small, dark spots and a short, coarse mane of hair on the back of its neck.

Hyenas can make many other sounds besides their "laugh." In fact, the creatures are among the noisiest of meat-eaters, with a large repertoire of calls. Hunting in a large pack led by a female, they make various whoops and yelps to keep in contact with each other as they scatter swiftly over the grasslands in search of food. Hyenas generally hunt at night, but it is not unusual to see them prowling cautiously about during the day, too. The hyenas will eat any meat that they find, dead or alive, but they most often make their own kill. Their tremendously strong jaws can crack through bone to get at the marrow inside. There is little left for the vultures when the hyenas are finished with their meal.

Can you find and color 12 mistakes?

10

Snow Leopard

Most great cats prowl steamy jungles or sun-drenched grasslands. The snow leopard, however, makes its home in the icy mountains of Central Asia. This large cat, also called the ounce, is well equipped for its wintry habitat. It has a beautiful thick coat of long, warm fur. Its pale coat is covered with dark spots—solid spots on its head and legs, and groups of spots, or rosettes, on the sides of its body and on its tail. The animal's tail is exceptionally long. A snow leopard with a four-foot-long body may have a three-foot-long tail.

The snow leopard is a solitary animal, although a female does sometimes take her cubs with her when she hunts. The cat preys upon musk deer, wild sheep and rodents, soundlessly stalking its victim, then pouncing from a rocky ledge when the time is right. The snow leopard roams between the tree line (the highest point at which trees can grow on the mountainside) and the snow line (the lowest level of the mountain where snow falls). In the summer, this cat may wander as high as three miles, or more than 15,000 feet, above the valley floor in search of food. The freezing winter sometimes drives the leopard down the mountains to about 6,500 feet. There, it sometimes preys on domestic animals such as goats. But the stealthy snow leopard is rarely seen or heard by humans.

Can you find and color 14 mistakes?

12

Giant Panda

The giant panda has an identity problem. Scientists can't decide whether the panda belongs in the bear family or the raccoon family. Some scientists think it belongs in a category of its own. Recent research on the animal's tooth structure and blood seems to favor it being a kind of bear.

The giant panda makes its home in cool, misty bamboo forests in the mountains of China. This animal munches up to 40 pounds of bamboo a day. It usually eats in a sitting position, gripping the bamboo between the pads of its clawed front feet.

The giant panda measures about five feet long from its nose to its stubby tail. It weighs a hefty 300 pounds or more. This chubby, playful animal is generally white with coarse black fur on its legs and shoulders. Round black ears and black patches around its eyes add to the giant panda's cuddly, stuffed-toy look. Newborn giant pandas are all white at birth, but their distinctive black patches on their legs and shoulders appear by the time they are one month old. At birth, the giant panda cubs weigh only about five ounces—less than a hamster! But the cubs grow quickly. Within eight weeks, they weigh 20 times their birthweight.

Can you find and color 15 mistakes?

Orangutan

Birds aren't the only animals that build nests in trees. The five-foot-tall, 200-pound orangutan builds a rough, leafy sleeping nest up to 80 feet from the ground. Even if it stays in the same area in its forest home for a while, the orangutan builds a new nest every night from leaves and strong branches. Before dropping off to sleep, it may cover its head and body with leaves, too. Orangutan nests have been discovered on the ground, but that is unusual. This tailless tree-dweller rarely abandons the safety of the branches except to reach another tree.

In the Malaysian language, *orang-utan* means "old man of the woods," and it's easy to see how the animal got its name. Older males have shaggy red hair, fat stomachs, cheek flaps, throat sacks and beards! Orangutans live in the forests of Borneo and Sumatra, dining on leaves and fruit. They will even occasionally eat birds' eggs, which are plentiful in the treetops. But the primates seem to prefer figs and a prickly, odd-smelling fruit called a durian (DOOR-ee-an). The orangutan's seven-foot-wide armspread and long fingers and toes make it easy for it to grip branches while stretching to pluck a tasty meal.

Can you find and color 12 mistakes?

Red Kangaroo

Can you imagine how big you would get if you grew throughout your entire life? That's what the red kangaroo does. An old male of 16 years or more can reach a length of nine feet from its long snout to the tip of its tail. The red kangaroo is the largest marsupial (mar-SOO-pee-ul). A marsupial is a type of mammal with a pouch or pocket on the belly of the female. A newborn kangaroo, about an inch long and weighing less than an ounce, crawls into its mother's pouch. There, it has a safe place to nurse and grow. The baby kangaroo will stay in its mother's pouch for about eight months, or until it is big enough to venture out on its own.

Red kangaroos rove the grasslands of Australia. They graze in small groups called mobs and are most active at night. In the heat of the day, they find a shady place to rest. When resting, a kangaroo may lean on its muscular tail as a prop. The tail is also important when the kangaroo is in a hurry. To reach top speed, the animal tilts forward, and, holding its slender forepaws up off the ground, it springs along on its exceptionally long hind legs with its tail held out behind for balance. The red kangaroo can race as fast as 40 miles per hour, leap more than 20 feet at a bound and clear a fence nine feet tall.

Can you find and color 15 mistakes?

Koala

Until it is about six months old, a baby koala cannot watch where it is going . . . only where it has been. That's because the pouch on its mother's tummy opens to the rear, unlike the pouch of the kangaroo. The fluffy-eared koala cub spends the first six months of life tucked safely in this pouch. When it is old enough, it rides on its mother's back as she moves slowly and carefully through the treetops.

The two-to-three-foot-long koala lives in the eucalyptus forests of Australia. This marsupial rarely comes to the ground. Its hands and feet are well designed for clinging to branches, with five clawed digits on each hand. Three of these "fingers" face forward and two face sideways, so that it looks as though the little creature has two thumbs.

The koala usually sleeps balanced in the fork of a tree during the day and is active at night. A very picky eater, it only eats the leaves of certain species of eucalyptus trees. And it doesn't come down for water. In fact, in the language of the Australian aborigines, *koala* means "one who does not drink." This cuddly looking animal gets all the water it needs from the more than two pounds of leaves it eats every day.

Can you find and color 15 mistakes?

Polar Bear

The polar bear is the swimming champion of the bear family. It lives along the icy Arctic coast and roams far out on the ice pack. This bear readily dives into the freezing water. A slow but strong swimmer, it can venture miles from shore, sometimes in search of a meal. Surprised sailors chanced across one polar bear swimming nearly 200 miles from shore, but that is an exception to the rule. A polar bear is more likely to stay within comfortable reach of the nearest shoreline or ice sheet. One of the world's largest meat-eaters, this hardy bear will eat walrus, fish and occasionally a large, leafy seaweed called kelp. Its main source of food, however, is seals. Although it is a good stalker, the polar bear usually simply sits near a breathing hole in the ice, waiting to catch a seal when it comes up for air.

The polar bear grows up to eight feet long, not counting its stubby tail, and over five feet high at the shoulder. Some males weigh as much as 1,500 pounds. Even so, the agile polar bear can run at about 25 miles per hour and can cover a distance of 12 feet in a single leap. Thick hair surrounding partially webbed foot pads helps the polar bear to keep its footing on the slippery ice.

How does this huge bear keep warm in its world of snow, ice and frigid water? It has a dense coat of pale fur, and the skin beneath its fur is black to better absorb the sun's warm rays. A thick layer of blubber beneath the polar bear's skin adds extra insulation, keeping this "lord of the Arctic" comfortable in its frozen domain.

Can you find and color 16 mistakes?

Grizzly Bear

The most dangerous thing about the grizzly is that it is unpredictable. This huge bear is generally peaceful by nature, but it may stand and attack if surprised or cornered, or if its cubs are threatened. The grizzly, however, is basically a loner, and it avoids contact with humans whenever possible.

The enormous grizzly bear is one of the largest bears in the world. A grizzly can weigh up to 900 pounds, and, with its thickly maned shoulder hump, scooped-in face and long, sharp fangs, it can look quite ferocious. Nearly four feet tall at the shoulder, this northern bear can tower more than seven feet tall when rearing up on its strong hind legs. This powerful mammal has huge front paws tipped with five-inch claws.

Unlike most bears, the short-tailed grizzly usually doesn't climb trees. It walks on all fours, with its padded, hairless heel and toes on the ground. It eats rodents, leaves, berries, fish and even grass. At one time, the grizzly roamed over most of North America. Now it can be found in large numbers only in forests in Alaska and parts of Canada. The decline of the grizzly bear has been caused by humans who, in the past, have hunted it and destroyed its habitat. Today, there are laws that protect the grizzly and its home.

Can you find and color 14 mistakes?

24

Timber Wolf

In a race, a timber wolf would not win a sprint, but it would do very well in a marathon. Trotting at a steady pace when tracking its prey, this largest member of the dog family can travel 40 miles or more without stopping for a rest! The timber wolf lives in the northern forests of the United States and Canada. Its thick coat of fur is usually gray, but it can be black, brown or rarely even pure white. This alert, intelligent animal looks much like a very large German shepherd.

Some wolves live alone, but most live and hunt in packs of up to 10 or more. Wolves will eat whatever they can catch, but they seem to prefer large prey, such as white-tailed deer, caribou and moose. The animals share a kill, and each can eat more than 20 pounds of meat at one meal.

Wolf packs are organized by rank and have a very strict social order. Scientists call the leader the "alpha" (meaning the first) male. All of the wolves in the pack obey him. Members of the pack communicate with snarls, growls, barks and yelps. A wolf has other ways of expressing itself, too. The muscles of its snout have a wide range of movement. It can change its facial expression and the position of its ears to show fear, anger or excitement.

Can you find and color 15 mistakes?

Wolverine

The wolverine is probably the most ferocious mammal of its size in North America. Little more than three feet long and weighing less than 50 pounds, this member of the weasel family seems absolutely fearless. Although the wolverine is generally a scavenger, it is able to overpower an animal much larger than itself, usually a weaker member of a herd of deer or moose. It has a tremendous appetite and the strong, bone-crushing teeth and powerful jaws to satisfy it. According to folklore, this tough little animal is said to eat more food pound for pound than any other meat-eater. Whether that is true or not, the wolverine is often called "the glutton." If it is hungry, this furry fury will drive another animal, even a mountain lion, from its kill in order to eat it.

The bushy-tailed wolverine lives in the northern forests of North America. Moving steadily in a clumsy gallop, it covers a hunting range of over 600 miles. Short-legged, stocky and wide, it is easy to recognize and rarely confused with other creatures in its range. The wolverine has a pale band of fur on each side of its dark, coarse coat and pale arcs of fur over its eyes. It is well adapted to its wintry habitat. The wolverine's unusual fur will not freeze, even if it gets wet. The wolverine's large, flat feet serve as a kind of snow shoe, preventing the animal from sinking in deep snow.

Can you find and color 14 mistakes?

American Bison

The first Europeans to gaze across the Great Plains of North America were met by an incredible sight. Huge herds of American bison, thousands of members strong, roamed there. As the herds moved, the ground rumbled and clouds of dust filled the air. For centuries, American Indians hunted the bison (also known as the buffalo) and carefully used the meat, skin, bones and even the tendons and horns, never wastefully decreasing their numbers. But the coming of the railroad spelled disaster for these beasts, as thoughtless hunters shot them from train windows, not even bothering to claim the meat. Thankfully, the attitude of the public changed as the American bison teetered on the brink of extinction. The small herds that are left are protected in special parks.

The American bison lives in open forests and on prairies, where it grazes on tough grasses. A little more than six feet high at its huge, powerful shoulders and nine feet long, a bison can weigh up to 2,000 pounds. Its shaggy coat is particularly full about its head, shoulders and forelimbs. Its short tail ends in a tuft of hair. The bison has a small pair of crescent-shaped horns on its head. During the mating season, the huge bulls clash head-first in battles for mates. It appears that the bison's tiny horns are not as helpful in deciding the winner as its hard skull. About nine months after mating, a female bison usually gives birth to a single calf. The American bison is a curious animal. When a calf is born, several adults may gather around to observe.

Can you find and color 14 mistakes?

30

Bighorn Sheep

In the Rocky Mountains of the United States and Canada, the sound of battling bighorn sheep can echo for miles. Each bighorn sheep has a pair of tough, coiled horns. The male uses its horns in contests of strength, perhaps to win a mate. Only individuals whose horns are of similar length will fight. The battle begins with two rival males shoving each other head to head. After a time, each backs off some distance. Then, as if at a signal, each animal rears up on its hind legs and charges at its rival. They meet with a resounding, headfirst crash.

The bighorn sheep is about four feet long from its nose to the tip of its short tail. The slender horns of a female are about eight inches long. A male's thick, heavy horns may reach three feet in length or more. The sheep's short, smooth coat is gray, with white patches at the stomach, rump, ears and on the snout.

The bighorn sheep is incredibly surefooted. Placing its hooves on the narrowest footholds, it easily trots up steep cliff faces out of the reach of enemies such as the wolf and mountain lion. Flocks of 20 animals or more may graze on mountain pastures or on patches of tough grass on a steep mountain slope.

Can you find and color 15 mistakes?

Northern Opossum

Have you ever pretended to be asleep when someone is talking to you? We call this "playing opossum," because the opossum often plays dead to escape its enemies. Many predators won't eat what they haven't killed themselves, and the northern opossum takes advantage of this. When cornered, it falls to the ground, its mouth gaping open, and lays still even when prodded. Once the attacker is convinced the opossum is dead, it gives up and moves on, and the opossum heads for safety.

With its pink nose and long, scaly tail, the northern opossum looks like a rat the size of a house cat. Its hairless ears are thin and papery. Long white hairs poke out from its dark fur, giving it a shaggy look. The northern opossum is the only marsupial in North America, and its young have one of the shortest developmental periods of any mammal. They are born less than two weeks after they are conceived! When the babies leave their mother's body, they cannot yet face the outside world. Blind and hairless, they climb through her fur to her pouch. Nine or ten week later, the babies are old enough to leave the pouch. As the mother waddles along in search of insects or fruit to eat, her young ride on her back, gripping her fur with their tiny pink paws. Soon, within six to eight months, these young, now adults, can give birth to their own offspring.

Can you find and color 15 mistakes?

34

Porcupine

The porcupine turns its back on its enemies. Known as "nature's pincushion," the porcupine protects itself with the sharp quills it has all over its back and tail. The crested porcupine of Africa turns its back on an attacker and rattles its hollow, one-foot-long quills in warning. If the warning is ignored, this porcupine charges backward toward its enemy. The North American porcupine simply bristles its nearly 30,000 quills at an attacker. It cannot "shoot" its quills, but with only a light touch the needles sink deeply into an inquisitive stranger's nose or paws. Lost or broken quills grow back. The porcupine is also covered by a soft undercoat of fur and long, spiky guard hairs. Because the quills are this animal's only line of defense, even baby porcupines are born with a full set. Fortunately for the female, who gives birth to one or two young at a time, her babies have soft quills that face backward during birth. These quills harden within half an hour.

A good tree climber, the 30-inch-long North American porcupine is a woodland rodent. It shuffles out at night to gnaw on plants and the inside layers of tree bark with its chisel-like teeth. Unfortunately for campers, it also chews on axe handles, canoe paddles and even car tires. One bold, although probably extremely near-sighted, porcupine waddled straight up to a forest ranger and began to gnaw on his boots!

Can you find and color 14 mistakes?

Nine-Banded Armadillo

The nine-banded armadillo is the only "armored" mammal in North America. Up to three feet long including its scaly tail, this animal has a protective shield of bony plates. Nine movable bands in the center of this stiff shield make it more flexible (in fact, the armadillo can curl into a ball!). Although its armor is a little heavy, the armadillo can swim very well. It swallows air to become more buoyant. When it prefers, it may choose to run across the bottom of a shallow stream instead of swimming. The nine-banded armadillo can hold its breath under water for up to six minutes.

This mammal also feels at home underground. With its sturdy claws it can dig a burrow five feet deep and 20 feet long or more, usually in a riverbank. The armadillo scrapes out the soil with its front feet, then its stout back feet kick the soil away. The animal can brace its tail against the tunnel floor to lift its hind feet so that they are able to move more freely. The nine-banded armadillo finds much of its food underground. Its sense of smell is so sharp that it can locate the worms and beetles it eats tunneling eight inches beneath the surface of the ground. This armadillo also eats roots, slugs, mice and even poisonous snakes.

Can you find and color 15 mistakes?

Giant Anteater

Although it has no teeth, the giant anteater does have a record-breaking tongue: It's almost two feet long! The anteater uses its sticky tongue to lick up ants and termites. It can easily devour more than 30,000 of these insects in a single day. The shaggy-furred giant anteater usually hunts during the day, finding its food by scent. Its sense of smell is at least 40 times more sensitive than a human's. With its very long snout to the ground, it carefully searches for a meal. When it finds an insect nest, it rips it open with the three sharp claws it has on each of its front feet. The longest claw may measure four inches, or about twice the length of your thumb. To protect its claws from wear, this creature walks on its thickly padded knuckles.

Nearly seven feet long and two feet tall at the shoulder, this animal is truly a giant among anteaters. Its very bushy tail makes up much of its length. The giant anteater lives in the swampy areas, open forests and grasslands of Central and South America. It can climb trees and swim well, but it lives mainly on the ground. The giant anteater is a loner, but it isn't unusual to see a female strolling along with her baby riding carefully on her back.

Can you find and color 12 mistakes?

Jaguar

The "great cats" are those that cannot purr but have a fearsome roar. They include the lion, cheetah, tiger, leopard and snow leopard of Asia and Africa. The only great cat in the Americas is the magnificent jaguar. Like the leopard, the jaguar has a short, black-spotted coat of orange fur. But it's not too difficult to tell them apart. The jaguar is heavier in build than the leopard and has a distinctive pattern of spots: Along its sides and back, its spots are arranged in groups of four or five in a ring around a central spot. It has solid spots on its head and neck and wide rings around the end of its tail. Like the leopard, on rare occasions all-black jaguars are born. The jaguar prowls forests and grasslands from Central to South America. The largest of these animals live in the south and may be almost six feet long, with a nearly three-foot-long tail.

The jaguar is a fine hunter. In the grasslands, it creeps up to its prey under the cover of tall grass. In the forest, it might climb a tree and pounce on a passing deer or tapir (a piglike animal the size of a donkey). An excellent swimmer, this big cat also catches fish and will even attack a crocodile. The jaguar seldom stakes out its territory far from a large river.

Can you find and color 13 mistakes?

Southern Elephant Seal

The largest of all the seals, the southern elephant seal can weigh as much as a mighty Indian elephant. Adult males can reach 20 feet long and have a foot-long, whiskered snout that looks a little like an elephant's trunk. Female seals have no trunk and are three or four times smaller than males.

The southern elephant seal lives in the Antarctic. It stays at sea for at least six months of the year, feeding on fish and squid. Although clumsy on land, this sea mammal is very graceful in the water. Steering with its front flippers, it whisks through the icy ocean with powerful strokes of its single tail flipper. Although the seal has a short coat of fur, its thick layer of blubber is what keeps it warm in the freezing waters. When at sea, the elephant seals may travel great distances. Scientists tagged and tracked one baby seal and discovered that it swam over 3,000 miles during the first year of its life!

In the fall, thousands of seals come ashore and form breeding colonies on the rocky islands and coasts of Antarctica and on the tip of South America. Each strong adult male claims a territory and gathers a harem of about 15 females, which he fiercely guards from other males.

Can you find and color 16 mistakes?

Answers

Page 3

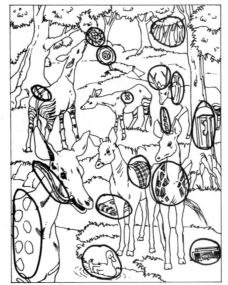

Page 5

Page 7

Page 9

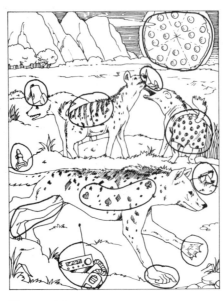

Page 11

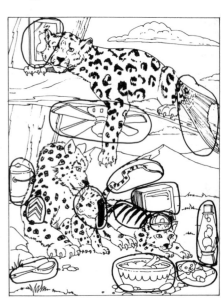

Page 13

Page 15

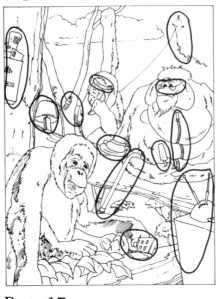

Page 17

Page 19

Page 21

Page 23

Page 25

Page 27

Page 29

Page 31

Page 33

Page 35

Page 37

Page 39

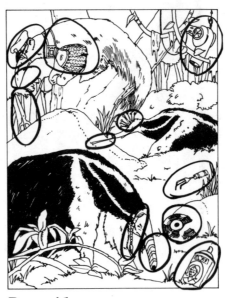

Page 41

Page 43

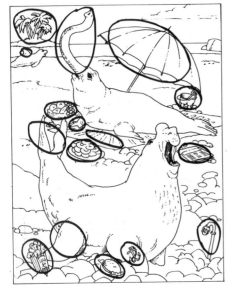

Page 45